The Two Giants

Retold by Mary Dickinson
Illustrated by Toni Goffe

Chapter 1

Long, long ago in the north there lived
a giant called Finn. Wherever he went,
Finn would say,
'I am the biggest and strongest giant
in the world.'

But in another land there lived a giant
called Culcullin. Wherever he went,
Culcullin would say,
'I am the biggest and strongest giant
in the world.'

Finn liked to juggle.

He also liked to do the garden.

And sometimes he liked to swim.

His wife Shaya was always there
to help him.

Culcullin had a magic little finger that made him strong.

Culcullin was so strong that he could catch lightning.

He could also hold back the clouds.

One day Culcullin heard about Finn,
the giant of the north, and he said,
'I will go and see him. I will show him
who is the strongest giant in the world.'

So Culcullin set off for the north.
He was so tall that his head was in
the clouds and he was so heavy
that as he walked he made
the road shake. As he went he sang,
'I'm coming to get you, Finn.
I'll break your bones and BASH you in.'

When Finn heard Culcullin coming he
said, 'Help! What am I going to do?
Culcullin has a magic finger and he is
much stronger than I am.'
'But he is not as clever as I am,' said
Shaya. 'Quick! Get into the baby's cot.'
So Finn climbed into the baby's cot.
Shaya put the baby's dummy in
his mouth and a hat on his head.
'Leave it to me,' she said.
'We will get his magic finger.'

Chapter 2

Culcullin walked up to Finn's house.
'Where is the giant called Finn?'
he shouted.
'Finn's not here,' said Shaya. 'There's
only the baby and me in the house.
But Finn will be back soon. You can
wait here for him.'
'I will,' said Culcullin. 'I want that
little Finn. I'll break his bones
and BASH him in.'

'Would you like a drink while you're waiting?' asked Shaya.

'Yes please,' said Culcullin.

'Then I need water,' said Shaya. 'Could you open up the mountain and find me a river?'

Culcullin looked surprised.

'Come, come,' laughed Shaya. 'Call yourself a giant? My Finn always finds me a river.'

'Oh, very well then,' said Culcullin, and with a HUFF and a PUFF he opened up the mountain and found a river. 'That was hard,' he said. 'Finn must be very strong.'

'Yes, I am,' said Finn quietly.

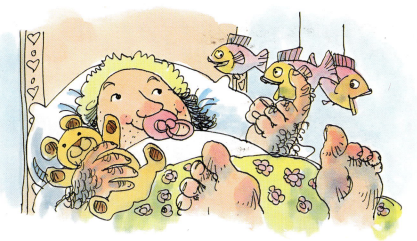

'Did I hear Finn?' shouted Culcullin.

'No, it was just the baby,' said Shaya.
'He must be getting hungry. I must cook
his dinner. Could you turn the house
round so the wind won't blow out
the fire?'

Culcullin looked surprised.

'Come, come,' laughed Shaya. 'Call
yourself a giant? My Finn always turns
the house round.'

'Oh, very well then,' said Culcullin,
and with a HUFF and a PUFF
he turned the house round.
'That was very heavy,' he said. 'Finn
must be very strong.'
'Yes, I am,' said Finn quietly.

'Did I hear Finn?' shouted Culcullin.

'No, it was only the baby,' said Shaya.

'He must be getting cold. Let's go inside.'

 So they went inside the house.

 Culcullin sat down by the fire.

'You must be hungry now,' said Shaya.

'I will make you a pie like the pies

 I make for Finn.'

'Thank you,' said Culcullin.

Chapter 3

Shaya made two pies. In one pie she put currants, and in the other she put stones. She put a cross on the top of the pie with the stones in. Then she put the pies in the oven. When they were cooked, Shaya gave Culcullin the pie with the cross on it.

Culcullin bit into the pie and his teeth
went CRUNCH on the stones.

'I can't eat this!' he shouted.

'Come, come,' laughed Shaya. 'Call
yourself a giant? My Finn always eats
his pie.'

'Oh very well then,' said Culcullin, and
he ate the pie.

'Ouch! My teeth hurt,' he cried.

'Good,' said Finn quietly.

'Did I hear Finn?' asked Culcullin.

'No,' said Shaya. 'It was only the baby.
He must be hungry. Could you give him
this pie?'

Culcullin sat down by the baby's cot.

He looked at Finn.

'What a big baby you are,' he said.

'Yes,' said Shaya. 'He is just like Finn. He is very big and very strong.'

'Can he eat the pie?' asked Culcullin.

'Oh yes,' said Shaya.

Culcullin put the pie in the baby's mouth and the baby ate it all up.

Culcullin was surprised.

'How does he do that?' he asked.

'He has very big teeth,' said Shaya.

'Put your little finger in his mouth and
feel his teeth. Put it right to the back.'

Culcullin put his little finger into
Finn's mouth.

When Culcullin's finger was right
at the back of his mouth, Finn bit it
so hard that he bit the finger right off.

'Give me back my finger,'
shouted Culcullin.

But Finn just smiled.

So Culcullin tried to open Finn's mouth,
but he wasn't strong any more.

'I want my finger. I want my finger,'
he said, and he started to cry.

'Sshhh,' said Shaya. 'Don't let Finn
hear you crying. Quick! Run away
before he comes home.'

So Culcullin ran all the way home
and never came back again.

When Culcullin had gone, Finn jumped out of the cot. He threw the finger away into the sea. Then he danced with Shaya around and around.

'Oh Shaya,' he said. 'You are the cleverest woman in the world. And I am the strongest giant in the world.'